sin to salvation

joe wells

*To our children: Colton, Michala, Camden,
and Bennett. Thank you for blessing our lives.
It is our earnest prayer that each of you will
faithfully follow Jesus Christ all of your life.
Your mother and I love you very much, and want
nothing more than for each of you to go to heaven.*

Sin to Salvation

Copyright © 2016 by Kaio Publications, Inc. All Rights Reserved.

All rights reserved. No portion of this book may be reproduced in any form for commercial purposes without the written permission of the Publisher.

Published by Kaio Publications, Inc.

5008 Guardian Ct.

Spring Hill, TN 37174

ISBN: 978-0-9960430-5-2

Unless noted otherwise Scripture is taken from NASB is taken from the New American Standard Bible, copyright © 1960, 1962, 1963, 1968, 1971, 1972, 1973, 1975, 1977, 1995 by The Lockman Foundation. Used by permission.

Book edited by Erin McDonald
Design and layout: D.J. Smith, Nashville, TN

Printed in the United States of America.

contents

	about joe	6
Chapter 1	sin entered the world	7
Chapter 2	god's response	15
Chapter 3	god's chosen people	23
Chapter 4	god's patience and love	29
Chapter 5	god offers atonement for sins	35
Chapter 6	the new is born	41
Chapter 7	the gospel is proclaimed	47
Chapter 8	new testament conversions	53
Chapter 9	saul's conversion	59
Chapter 10	cornelius' conversion	65
Chapter 11	what must i do to be saved?	71
Chapter 12	now that i'm saved, what's next?	79
Chapter 13	what will that day be like?	85

about joe

Joe Wells holds an earned B.S. degree in Science along with a completion certificate from the Nashville School of Preaching and Biblical Studies and a Masters of Ministry degree from Freed Hardeman University. Joe travels the country as a frequent speaker for youth and family events. He is the co-founder of Kaio Publications, publishers of the *Family Devotional* series as well as other great resources. Joe is also the author of the book *Game Plan: Developing a Spiritually Winning Strategy for Adults and Teens in Today's Culture*. Joe has served God in a public way since 2000 in the capacity of youth minister and gospel preacher, helping people make the connection with the Word of God and encouraging them to be transformed for Christ. Joe and his wife Erin, along with their four children, Colton, Michala, Camden, and Bennett, reside in Spring Hill, Tennessee.

chapter 1:
sin entered the world

introduction

Tonight's game was the first opportunity in eight years for the Bears to be state champions. Captain Wheeler Jordan determined that this game had to be the best. "Three of us are playing our last high school game," he told his excited team, as the referee's whistle sounded to begin the game. "We're going to be champs again. We're going to win this game whatever the cost!" As the team broke huddle, Wheeler raised his voice: "Whatever the cost!"

And what a game it was! Neither team led by more than five points at any time during the game, and the lead had alternated eleven times. The Bears, ahead by two points with 40 seconds to play, switched to a man-to-man defense.

Then the inevitable happened. The Tigers' guard, Shorty Thomas—who would have thought it!—sunk a long, uncoordinated three-pointer. Wheeler was delirious and quickly signaled to the referee. "Time out—Bears!" The announcer's tense voice boomed, hardly audible above the roar of the Bears' home crowd.

The Bears' Coach Bo Jo set up what he hoped would be the final play of the game. "Lefty, throw the ball in—to anyone open. Charlie, you stay outside. The ball's coming to you; you can get it inside to Dead-Eye." Coach Jo slapped Dead-Eye, one of the seniors, on the back. "The game is in your hands."

The Bears pounced back onto the floor. Lefty inbounded the ball and Nerdie swatted it to Charlie in the backcourt. The clock ticked…33, 32, 31. Dead-Eye started for the goal, hands held high. So far, so good.

But who could have guessed what would have happened next?

Yes, Charlie hurled the ball in the right direction, but when a Tiger player dove for it, it ricocheted off his fingers and fell into Nerdie's hands. Dead-Eye, hoping to draw the foul instead of Nerdie, lunged toward the ball. At the same time, every Tiger player ran toward Nerdie with a passion—almost like a football game. Although confusion ruled, the referee called a foul against the Tigers.

As the pile unraveled, sorting things out was not easy. After all, Dead-Eye and Nerdie were near each other when the foul occurred, and they were similar in stature. Captain Wheeler grabbed Nerdie by the shoulder and whispered forcefully, "Stand back!" Then he gave Dead-Eye a slap on the back. "Go to the line!" The excitement of the Tigers players was far too great for logic. The Tigers spectators were screaming, sensing some subtle violation. The Tigers' coach was on the verge of a heart attack yelling and waving for an official time-out. The referee warned of technical foul, so the crowd quieted. As Dead-Eye came to the foul line, the Tigers lined up to grab the ball just in case the best free-throw shooter in the state happened to miss…but Dead-Eye didn't miss. With three seconds left to play, the visitors were crazy with rage. The scorekeeper faithfully registered the score: Bears 88; Tigers 87.

Pandemonium reigned in the bleachers—the Bears fans, in their great excitement at having wrestled the game from the Tigers; the Tigers fans, sensing they were being cheated out of the greatest game they would ever see.

The frantic Tigers were waiting to put the ball into play and try for one last impossible basket. The referee, ball in hand stopped suddenly; the sound of his whistle somehow pierced the roar of the crowd. Three seconds left to play and the referee calls official time? The two officials met for an instant; the referee pointed to Dead-Eye and waved his arms in a scissor-like motion. In the complete silence of the moment, the announcer said: "Ladies and gentlemen, the wrong player was at the foul line. The baskets did not count." The scorekeepers readjusted the score: Bears 86; Tigers 87.

The bleachers exploded—instantaneously. As the Tigers threw the ball in, Tigers fans counted down to the defeat of the Bears—"3, 2, 1. Number one! number one! number one! We're number one!" Tigers fans shouted again and again.

The Bears, heads down, shuffled toward the dressing room. Wheeler walked with his face in his hands. Bears fans, many of them tearfully trying to find an exit, knew their opponents were telling the truth. The Bears had almost cheated their way to victory, but might is not always right, winning is not equal to championship, deceit never pays.

There was an especially bitter pill the Bears had to swallow, a pill that would choke Wheeler for a long time. Had Wheeler not gone against the rule, Nerdie just might have scored the winning baskets.

lesson summary

Today's lesson is about God's directions that He gave to Adam and Eve in the Garden of Eden. We will see how they failed to follow the rules God gave them and, as a result, "lost the game." We will begin our study through *Sin to Salvation* at the very beginning.

text

In the book of Genesis chapter 1 verse 26 & 27, we read of how God created humans:

"Let Us make man in Our image, according to Our likeness; and let them rule over the fish of the sea and over the birds of the sky and over the cattle and over all the earth, and over every creeping thing that creeps on the earth (NASB)."

It's this human, created in the image of God, we find when we turn over to Genesis 2:7 who is being placed in the most beautiful garden with all the food he could ever imagine, other than chocolate cake. We don't read in the Bible that was there; however, beside cake, he had all the food he really needed to live and enjoy the beautiful creation God had given him. It is crystal clear that by God doing this, placing Adam in the richest place he created, He wanted to give him the absolute best.

With many of the gifts from God, He often also gives boundaries that are to be followed if a person is going to be allowed to enjoy the gift to the fullest. Being placed in the Garden of Eden was no exception. That's why we read God telling Adam, *"From any tree of the garden you may eat freely; but from the tree of knowledge of good and evil you shall not eat, for in the day that you eat from it you will surely die* (Gen. 2:16, 17)."

Now, as the pages turn a little and Adam realizes there is not another human for him relationally, we read of the account of God creating Eve. As you may already know, God causes Adam to fall into a deep sleep, and He then takes a rib from Adam and forms the first woman. Their job was to cultivate and keep the garden (Gen. 2:15). However, they also had a responsibility to keep the commandment from God about not eating from the tree of knowledge of good and evil. They could enjoy the fruit from any of the other trees, but not this one special tree that was out of bounds for them.

Doesn't this sound like it would be the perfect life? Man has been created in the image of God. He has been placed in a beautiful garden that has wonderful trees, food, water, and beauty all around. God has created woman to be a helper and a companion to man, and together they are to live happy ever after. What a wonderful life it would be if only the account would have stopped here!...But, you and I both know it doesn't.

As we continue reading in Genesis chapter 3:1, we are introduced to a serpent that the Bible describes as, "*...more crafty than any beast of the field which the Lord God has made.*" It's this crafty one who comes to Eve and asks her about what God had said concerning eating from the tree of knowledge of good and evil. Eve tells him that they are not to eat of the tree or else they will die. To which the serpent replies, "*You surely will not die! For God knows that in the day you eat from it your eyes will be opened, and you will be like God, knowing good and evil*" (Gen. 3:4, 5).

The serpent tells Eve one of the biggest lies ever known when he tells her that God doesn't really mean what He says, but rather He just doesn't want her to be like Him. The sad thing is, Eve falls for it and eats of the tree. It doesn't stop there, because we find that Eve then brings the fruit to Adam who also eats some of it. We see an immediate change in Adam and Eve. The Bible records that, *"the eyes of both of them were opened, and they knew that they were naked; and they sewed fig leaves together and made themselves loin coverings. They heard the sound of the Lord God walking in the garden in the cool of the day, and the man and his wife hid themselves from the presence of the Lord God among the trees of the garden* (Gen. 3:7, 8)." Sin, going beyond the boundaries God had set, really did make a difference. Things really did change.

lessons learned

The human side of Adam and of Eve really came out in this account of the first sin recorded in the Bible. The serpent, the devil, is no beginner. He knew the weakness of Eve, and he knows our weaknesses today. He knows how to get to you and he is very good at what he does. He will tell you a lie and make it sound so attractive that it will make you take a second look at what God has said. He did it to Eve, and he's still using this same method of attack today.

As we look at the situation that happened with Adam and Eve, we need to carefully consider two very important lessons we can learn.

chapter 1: sin entered the world   13

1) If we sin, God knows, even if no one else does.

In the Garden of Eden, we only find two humans, Adam and Eve; a serpent; and then God. Adam and Eve sinned, but they didn't go around broadcasting it to God on a radio. However, God still knew that they were guilty of sinning against Him by eating of the tree of knowledge of good and evil.

2) We can't hide from God.

We find Adam and Eve trying to hide from God when they hear Him coming through the garden. They couldn't hide. We read of this quality of God in Psalm 147:5, *"Great is our Lord and abundant in strength; His understanding is infinite."* There is nothing that restricts God. He sees our hearts and knows our thoughts. We can't hide from God.

recap

For me to say, "I don't know why people sin" would not be true. Often times, we go outside of the boundaries God sets because we are very selfish. We want what we want, and we want it right now. It's this way of thinking that caused Wheeler to send Dead-Eye to the line instead of Nerdie. He was the one who was really fouled, but Wheeler's desire took over, and he thought he would be able to hide the truth and sell a lie. In the end, the defeat hurt even more because they really cheated themselves out of a chance to win the game.

In life, you are going to be faced with some tough choices. God has given us His directions in His Word because He loves us and wants us to be in heaven. He really does want to bless us beyond what we could ever imagine. However, just like in the opening basketball game, if we are going to enjoy the sweet taste of victory, we must stay within the boundaries God has set. Adam and Eve failed to do so, and it cost them dearly. When you and I think we can sin and "get-away-with-it," we are only fooling ourselves. God still knows.

questions for thought

1. What are some struggles with sin that teens around you are having?
2. Why do you think people try to deny their sins and cover them up?
3. What happens within you when you try to hide sin?
4. Instead of hiding our sins, what is the way that God wants us to handle our sins?
5. Why is it so difficult for teens, and adults, to handle their sins the way that God wants?

chapter two:
God's response

introduction

Nellie is a young lady who loves clothes, and she loves to shop and help others coordinate their outfits…and she has a good eye for it. She and her friend, Sarah, had grown up together and always saw eye-to-eye when it came to the subject of boys and the way a young lady should act towards them, and especially the way a young lady should dress around them. However, as they grew older, things began change.

"I can't wait until I can get a boyfriend," Sarah would say regularly as she seemed to reach a phase of being infatuated with boys. We would call that "boy-crazy" today, and truth be told, it seemed to become Sarah's identity. All she ever wanted to talk about was whether or not this guy or that guy would text her or want to chat. Nellie is a typical young lady who is also attracted to boys; however, there was a growing gulf between the way Sarah talked about them and the way Nellie viewed them.

One day, as Sarah and Nellie were out shopping, Sarah noticed a blouse (for the guys that means a shirt) that just stood out to her. She wanted it so bad and even tried it on. "I definitely love the color and design on you," said Nellie offering her feedback. "The only thing I don't like about it is that it is extremely low and it shows too much skin," Nellie continued honestly. "Oh…come on. You and I both know it looks good, and besides, we are growing up and our clothes will have to 'grow-up' with us," Sarah replied ignoring Nellie's attempt to keep modesty in the forefront.

Not having the money to get the shirt, Sarah changed out of the shirt and returned it to the rack. As they left, Nellie– being the person who loves to help coordinate outfits– made a mental note of the blouse and began brainstorming ideas as to how to make it work for her good friend.

After Nellie dropped Sarah off at home, she decided to go back to the store and buy the blouse for a birthday present for her good friend. However, she had already figured out that if she layered the blouse with an undershirt, then Sarah would have no problem wearing the one she really liked. So Nellie bought both shirts and quickly went home to wrap them for the special day.

The next week, at Sarah's birthday party, Nellie was so excited to give this special gift to her friend. "Open the yellow one!" her friends said giggling. "Wow!! I love it," Sarah exclaimed as she grinned from one side of her face to the other. "Nellie, thank you so much. You know exactly what I want. You are such a great friend!" Sarah said as she hugged Nellie– which made Nellie feel so rewarded and appreciated because she had put a lot of thought into this gift.

Later that night, the girls decided they were going to go out to dinner and then to a movie together. As they all met at Sarah's house, they were greeted by the birthday girl wearing her new shirt. The only problem was, Sarah had decided to not wear the undershirt that was purchased to make the outer shirt modest. Nellie felt so uncomfortable. She knew why she gave both shirts as a gift, and based upon the conversation she had with Sarah at the store, she assumed Sarah knew as well.

"Sarah, before we leave, can I speak with you for a minute?" Nellie asked. "Sure, what's up?" Sarah replied. "I'm confused," Nellie began. "When you tried on that shirt in the store, I told you that it was too low cut and would show too much. That's why I gave you the other shirt along with it. So you could layer the two. Why aren't you wearing the other shirt with it?" Nellie's managed to ask as her voice began to crack, unsure how her good friend would take her question. "Oh Nellie, I told you, we are growing up and it's okay for our clothes to 'grow-up' with us. This is fine, and besides, you picked the absolutely right shirt out for me. I know I'll get the guys attention tonight," Sarah replied as she walked back into the main room where the rest of the girls were waiting.

Nellie decided not to go that night. She felt so sad as she realized she and Sarah were no longer on the same page. She regretted ever buying that shirt, wishing there were some way to take it back.

lesson summary

In today's lesson we are going to study about God's response to a sinful world. We read that He was actually sorry He had made man (Gen. 6: 6, 7). We are going to look at how He handled it and why.

text

We read in Genesis 6: 5-7, "*Then the Lord saw that the wickedness of man was great on the earth, and that every intent of the thoughts of his heart was only evil continually. The Lord said, 'I will blot out man whom I have created from the face of the land, from man to animals to creeping things and to birds of the sky; for I am sorry that I have made them.'*"

From this passage we learn there was wickedness in man, and that God was sorry that He had made man. We do find that there was one man who found favor in the sight of God. (Gen. 6:8) His name was Noah. The Bible goes on to describe Noah in Gen. 6:9 in the following ways:

- A righteous man
- Blameless in his time
- Noah walked with God

Before we can continue, it is important for us to understand what these qualities mean.

"Righteous" - being up to a standard of right or just

"Blameless" - complete or mature

"Walked with God" - process of living life one step at a time in a close personal relationship with God, the creator

(There is another man we read of in Genesis 5:24 by the name of Enoch who also walked with God. Both of these men are remembered by their faith in the book of Hebrews chapter 11 verses 5-7.)

It is because Noah found favor in God's sight that He told Noah of His plan to destroy the earth and the people on it.

"*The end of all flesh has come before Me; for the earth is filled with violence because of them; and behold, I am about to destroy them with the earth*" (Gen. 6:13).

God went on to tell Noah He wanted an ark built that was (Gen. 6:14-16)

1. made out of gopher wood
2. with individual rooms,
3. covered inside and outside with pitch
4. 300 cubits (450 ft) in length
5. 50 cubits (75 ft) in width
6. 30 cubits (45 ft) tall
7. A window was to be placed in the ark and finish it to a cubit (18 in.) from the top.
8. with a door on the side
9. there were to be 3 decks (lower, second, third)

God then told Noah He was to gather animals and bring them along. In chapter 7 verses 2-3 we read, "*You shall take with you of every clean animal by sevens, a male and his female; and of the animals that are not clean two, a male and his female; also of the birds of the sky, by sevens, male and female, to keep offspring alive on the face of all the earth.*"

You might be wondering what makes an animal clean or unclean. It does not have anything to do with whether or not they took a shower that day. It has to do with the physical features the animals had. The clean animals were used in sacrifices and other religious events.

It rained for 40 days and all the earth was flooded. All the evil at that time was destroyed.

lessons learned

1) Sin makes God sad.

Have you ever wondered if God has emotions? Sadness is an emotion just the same as happiness or anger. God tells us in His Word He was *"grieved to His heart"* (Gen. 6:6). While we know God is spirit and not flesh (John 4:24), it is important to note the Scripture does teach about God in human terms as the writers, inspired by the Holy Spirit, reveal various qualities of God. One of these is the talk of God's heart and the effect of our sin on Him. We read in the New Testament in Romans 6:23 that, *"For the wages of sin is death, but the free gift of God is eternal life in Christ Jesus our Lord."* Now, the death talked about here is not a physical death, but rather a spiritual death. Sin separates you from God, and that makes Him sad.

2) There were some spared.

One of the interesting facts about the account of the flood is that Noah and his family were saved because they were the only ones who were doing what they were supposed to in the sight of God (Gen. 7:1). In the world in which we live, there are plenty of people walking around who are living in sin. I am sure you know some in your schools or on your sports team who are living a way that is not considered "righteous" in the sight of God. You might even be in this condition right now yourself. You need to know:

1. Sin does make God sad, and it separates you from Him

2. There were some spared, but they were the ones who were living the way God wanted them to live.

recap

Disappointments happen. At times those disappointments will come from the way other people act, and at other times disappointments will come from the way we, individually, act. Nellie never intended for Sarah to use the gift she gave her for bad, but Sarah always had that option. It didn't change Nellie's goodness and pureness in her gift-giving. It simply points to the freedom Sarah has as a person who makes her own decisions.

God made us as what is called "free-moral agents." That simply means He didn't make you a robot. He gave you the freedom to choose to follow Him or not. That's a demonstration of His goodness. However, with this gift comes the reality that not all people will choose to be obedient to God's will with this gift. When we choose to follow our own desires instead of God's will, we bring grief to God. The opposite of this is true as well. The Holy Spirit inspired the apostle John to say as much when he wrote, *"I have no greater joy than this, to hear of my children walking in the truth"* (1 John 3:4).

questions for thought

1. Does God really care if you are separated from Him?
2. Do you really care if you are separated from Him?

3. Why do you think people struggle with using their free will to be obedient?

4. If you ever found yourself in Nellie's shoes, how would you have responded to Sarah?

5. Imagine you knew God was going to destroy the world tomorrow. Name one person who you would talk with about changing his life to fit what God wants. What would you tell him?

Chapter Three:
God's chosen people

introduction

    The stakes couldn't be any higher. In the junior high boy way, Eric had challenged Ted to a pick-up game of football. The winner would take all the glory and bragging rights that came with being able to back up their boasting. As the guys began to assemble to pick teams, Ted's cousin, Dustin, came up to him and said, "Ted, man you know I'm always picked last. Please promise me that if you have a chance to pick me, you will. I know I can help you win this game." Ted thought to himself quietly, "Dustin is one of the smallest guys out here, and if I pick him all the other guys will give me a hard-time. Plus, he's not that good. However, he is my cousin, and that has to mean something." Looking back at Dustin, Ted replied, "Okay, if I have the opportunity to pick you, I will before the selecting is over." Dustin was so appreciative.

    "Sean," "Rusty," "Kevin," the boys said as they alternated between picks. "Blake," "Colton," "Camden," "Bennett," they continued until finally there was one boy left…Dustin. It was Ted's pick since Eric selected first, so Dustin began to take a step toward his cousin's team, so happy he was on Ted's team. "Wait a minute!" another boy named Tom yelled as he came running over. "I had to finish up the chores my mom asked me to do before I could come out and play," Tom said through his heavy breathing due to the fact he had just run from his house to the field. "Okay, Dustin step back over there. Ted, it's your pick," Eric replied, knowing he was going to get stuck with Dustin.

Ted, knowing that Tom was one of the best players out of the bunch, looked at both boys. "If I pick Tom, I know my team will be much stronger and faster. I just know he will help my team win," Ted thought to himself. "But what about my promise to Dustin? I did tell him I would pick him. I don't want him to think of me as a liar and one who doesn't stick to his promises," Ted, weighing the choice, contemplated.

Opening his mouth, Ted yelled out, "I choose Dustin." Dustin's eyes lit up and he began to grin from one ear to the next. Unfortunately, the other boys grinned as well, but it wasn't for the same reasons. They began to laugh and point at Ted. "What!?!" one boy exclaimed. "What are you doing?" another said as he laughed.

Ted looked at Dustin, and then he looked at the other guys laughing. All he could think to himself was that he had just thrown the game away. Tom was definitely the better, more talented player. However, the more he stared at Dustin, the more he began to feel comfortable with his pick, because it was about something bigger than the bragging rights or the ability to tell Eric how much better he was at football. It was about integrity and honesty. This pick was about being a man who keeps his word.

As the guys divided up and went to opposite sides of the ball, Dustin looked at Ted and shook his head as if to say, "Thank you for making me feel valued." Ted looked back nodding his head as if to gesture, "You're welcome," assured he had just done the right thing.

Chapter 3: God's chosen people

lesson summary

In today's lesson we are going to learn about a promise God made to a man named Abraham. This promise was never broken, because, unlike some of our friends or family, God doesn't break promises. He didn't then, and He doesn't today.

text

We begin lesson three at the point where Abraham is going to sacrifice his promised son, Isaac, to the Lord because that is what the Lord had commanded him to do in Genesis 22:2. Abraham does just as the Lord commands him to do, and just as he is about to sacrifice Isaac, the angel of the Lord stops him. We find that the Lord provids a ram instead for the burnt offering. It is here where we pick up the text in Genesis 22:15-19. We read:

Then the angel of the LORD called to Abraham a second time from heaven, and said, "By Myself I have sworn, declares the LORD, because you have done this thing and have not withheld your son, your only son, indeed I will greatly bless you, and I will greatly multiply your seed as the stars of the heavens and as the sand which is on the seashore; and your seed shall possess the gate of their enemies. 'In your seed all the nations of the earth shall be blessed, because you have obeyed My voice." So Abraham returned to his young men, and they arose and went together to Beersheba; and Abraham lived at Beersheba.

It is this promise God made to Abraham that results in the people that we know as the Israelites. We know Abraham has a son named Isaac, and we also know that Isaac has two sons: Jacob and Esau. It is through Jacob from which the 12 tribes of Israel come.

It is very important that you see the promise that was made to Abraham. God is very unique in His keeping of promises. I am sure you have had promises made to you in the past that were broken at one time. You felt horrible. You might have even felt used and gullible for falling into the broken promise. That is the neat thing about God, when He says it, you can believe it. He has a perfect record of keeping His promises.

We can see this perfect record in the events of Jacob and his wrestling with God (Gen. 32: 24-32). Jacob's name is changed to Israel, and God makes a promise to him in Genesis 35: 9-12.

Then God appeared to Jacob again when he came from Paddan-aram, and He blessed him. God said to him, *"Your name is Jacob; You shall no longer be called Jacob, But Israel shall be your name."* Thus He called him Israel. God also said to him,

"I am God Almighty; Be fruitful and multiply; A nation and a company of nations shall come from you, And kings shall come forth from you. "The land which I gave to Abraham and Isaac, I will give it to you, And I will give the land to your descendants after you."

We know that Israel (Jacob) does have 12 sons and that one of those sons, Joseph, is sold into slavery. It is because God was with him that Joseph makes it to a high official in Egypt, and it is because of this that the 12 tribes of Israel make it into Egypt.

We can read about the children of Israel as they wander in the wilderness, as they build the tabernacle, as they go through the period of the 13 judges, the time of the kings, and all the rest of the way through their history and we can see God still keeping His promise. He promises Abraham that he will be the father of a multitude, and God also promises Abraham that his people will overcome their enemies. God promises Jacob that a great nation will come from him, kings will come from his people, and that He will give to Jacob and his descendants the land that was promised to Abraham. You know, in both cases, God followed through with His promises.

lessons learned

1) God keeps His promises.

As teenagers, you are living in a world that promises a lot of things. You are constantly faced with them in the TV programs that you watch: promises of acceptance, or popularity, or happiness with money or alcohol. Unfortunately, the record of kept promises versus broken promises is not good. The broken ones outweigh the kept ones.

Aren't you glad that God is not of this world? I know sometimes we want to think of Him in human ways, but He is divine. That means He is greater than human ways. He does not let us down, and He doesn't break promises.

2) God has made a promise to people today.

Romans 6: 23 - *"For the wages of sin is death, but the free gift of God is eternal life in Christ Jesus our Lord."*

God has promised that sin will produce death. Like we talked about last chapter, this death is not a physical death, but rather a spiritual separation from God. However, He doesn't stop there. He continues to say that there is a free gift available: eternal life in Christ Jesus our Lord. We read in Matthew 25: 46, *"These will go away into eternal punishment, but the righteous into eternal life."* There is promise of eternal life for those who are in right-standing with God!

recap

When you think about it, Ted had to go against what regular, every day culture says by picking Dustin for his team. With so much on the line, at least in the mind of the junior high guys, Ted was willing to stick to his word and risk losing a game. In the end, winning or losing a game doesn't really matter; however, being a person who keeps his promises does matter.

That's what we see from our God. He makes promises throughout His Word, and He keeps them. Unlike what we experience in our world today, God has a perfect record of kept promises, and you and I can expect God to be consistent with the promises He's made concerning our eternity. What a blessing! When God says it, He means it.

questions for thought:

1. What do you think the response from your parents would be if you didn't keep a promise you made? Consequences?

2. How much trust do you have in someone who continually breaks promises?

3. What if you could be on the side of one who never breaks a promise? Would you join that side? Why?

4. Knowing that God has a perfect record of kept promises, why would you not want to join Him?

chapter four
God's patience and love

introduction

"That's it!" Julie thought. "I've had enough".

She grabbed the dirty sweater and forcefully marched down the hall right to her sister's room. Standing in the doorway, sweater in one hand and the other curled into a fist, Julie yelled, "Did you come into my room, take my sweater out of the closet and wear it?"

Michala looked up from the book she was reading with a surprised expression on her face and replied, "I sure did!" "You come into my room all the time and take my clothes and never think anything's wrong with it," Michala said very defensively, yet attacking. "Why do you have such a big problem with me doing it if you think it's okay for you to do the same?"

Julie's blood began to boil as the anger grew inside of her. All she wanted to do was go over to Michala and unleash her fury; however, she never left the door. She simply stared at her sister, waiting for the right words to come to her that would put a stop to this injustice.

"You're right", Julie said. "I shouldn't have come into your room and worn your clothes, but if you felt what I did was wrong, why did you do the same to me?" she asked. "I won't come in to your room and borrow your clothes without asking anymore, but I'm going to ask you show me the same curtesy," Julie said opting for a more diplomatic and calm response than she felt.

"Fine!" I'm sorry I wore your sweater without asking," Michala said hoping Julie would leave her alone so she could get back to her book. Being satisfied and feeling good that she hadn't acted on her first response, Julie turned and walked away from her sister's door, stopping to place the sweater in the dirty clothes hamper along the way.

lesson summary

In today's lesson we are going to look at God's response to the children of Israel. They were constantly doing things which would drive a person crazy and respond in a very human way, but we are going to look at how God responds.

text

We all remember the story of the children of Israel in the land of Egypt. They are almost beaten and worked to death, and they cry out to God and He hears them. God calls Moses from the burning bush (Ex. 3:2) and tells him to go to Egypt and demand that God's people be set free. After some excuses, Moses goes to Pharaoh and demands *"Let My People Go."* At this point we run into Pharaoh's refusal and the ten plagues.

1. Water to Blood (Ex. 7:17)
2. Swarms of Frogs (Ex 8:2)
3. Swarms of Gnats (Ex 8:16)

4. Swarms of Insects (Ex 8:21)
5. Death to Egyptian Livestock (Ex 9:3)
6. Boils upon the people (Ex. 9:9)
7. Hail comes down (Ex. 9:18)
8. Swarms of locust (Ex. 10:4)
9. Darkness comes upon Egypt (Ex. 10:21)
10. Death of all firstborn (Ex. 11:5)

It is at this point we begin to find out about the children of Israel, and their lack of confidence in God. In Exodus chapter 14 verses 11 and 12 we read, *"Then they said to Moses, 'Is it because there were no graves in Egypt that you have taken us away to die in the wilderness? Why have you dealt with us in this way, bringing us out of Egypt? Is this not the word that we spoke to you in Egypt, saying, 'Leave us alone that we may serve the Egyptians'? For it would have been better for us to serve the Egyptians than to die in the wilderness."*

This is their statement to Moses as they are standing before the Red Sea. They are watching as Pharaoh's men are approaching very quickly. They are afraid, but instead of trusting in God to deliver them, they doubt. What gets me is they have just finished watching the 10 plagues God had brought down upon Egypt. They have seen His power and love for them, but now as they face what they see as trouble, they doubt and complain.

We continue to see God's chosen people complain throughout the wilderness journey. However, no matter how much they complain, God always provides for their needs. *"So the people grumbled at Moses, saying, 'What shall we drink?' Then he cried out to the Lord, and the Lord showed him a tree; and he threw it into the water, and the waters became sweet"* (Exodus 15:24, 25).

Exodus 16:3: *"The sons of Israel said to them, 'Would that we had died by the Lord's hand in the land of Egypt, when we sat by the pots of meat, when we ate bread to the full; for you have brought us out into this wilderness to kill this whole assembly with hunger.' Then the Lord said to Moses, 'Behold, I will rain bread from heaven for you; and the people shall go out and gather a day's portion every day, that I may test them, whether or not they will walk in My instruction."*

As the children of Israel continued to wander in the wilderness, they continue to complain and doubt they will be taken care of. It seems to me this group of people, whom God had rescued time and time again, would have gotten the picture by now; however, we find that is not the case.

When the children of Israel came to Mt. Sinai, Moses went up on the mountain (Ex. 24:18). We read in the next few chapters of the instructions God gives to Moses for His people. While Moses is up on the mountain, the children of Israel begin, once again, to complain and doubt. They came to Aaron and had him build an idol for them to worship. (Ex. 32: 1)

This angered God and He wanted to destroy the people (Ex. 32: 10). However, Moses reminds Him of the promise He had made to Abraham, and we find where God changes His mind. (Ex. 32: 14)

lessons learned

1) God is patient.

Parents have to be very patient with children because they mess up in their learning. Can you imagine if a parent was not patient and decided they were going to expect perfection from their baby? Do you really think that the baby could, at that stage, do everything perfectly? Of course not, they are still learning.

Just like God in dealing with His children then, He is patient with us today. We read in 2 Peter 3:9, *"The Lord is not slow about His promises, as some count slowness, but is patient toward you, not wishing for any to perish but for all to come to repentance."*

2) God is Love.

John 3:16, 17: *"For God so loved the world that He sent His only begotten Son, that whoever believes in Him shall not perish, but have eternal life. For God did not send His Son into the world to judge the world, but that the world might be saved through Him."*

God loves you much more than you will ever understand. He sent His Son, Jesus, to die on the cross, which was a death so cruel it was reserved for the worst criminals. That is how much He loves you. Now let me ask you: How much do you love Him?

recap

Let's face it, there are times when our first response is not always the best. When we encounter difficult or uncomfortable circumstances, the response we give reveals our true character. Are we quick to lash out? Physically attack? Or shy away and hide? As we continue to grow and become more like Christ, we must grow to reflect and mimic our Heavenly Father's responses to everyone.

questions for thought

1. When parents discipline their child, does it mean they don't love that child?

2. Read and discuss the listing the Lord gives describing Himself in Exodus 34:6-7.

3. Discuss the patience and love of God in our lives.

4. How do you reflect the love and patience of God in your dealings with other teens in the classroom, cafeteria, ball field, etc.?

chapter five:
God offers atonement for sins

introduction

As we begin this chapter, think about each one of the following scenarios, and then answer the questions at the end.

1. Bill has been working in the grocery store for 2 months. He seems to be a good employee; however, Bill has been stealing money from the cash register. His boss suspects him, but is not sure. What would be the right thing for Bill to do?

2. Tommy loves his new game he got for his birthday. His friend down the street really likes it too; however, his friend didn't get one for his birthday. One day Tommy's game turns up missing. His friend took it, but Tommy doesn't know that. What would be the right thing for his friend to do?

3. In math class one day, you realize that you have forgotten to do the homework from the night before. The teacher tells the class at the end of the period to lay your paper by the door on your way out. You don't have yours done; however, your friend who is sitting right next to you is trying to show you

hers so you can copy. You end up copying, and you hand it in. Have you done the right thing, and how can you make right the wrong that was done?

Each of these case studies carries with it what is called a "dilemma." A dilemma is when a situation occurs because of circumstances that were either created by you or by others. This situation usually requires a decision to be made that could either make the situation better or worse, and at times, a decision will make the situation both better and worse, depending upon which side of the situation you are on.

In all, the goal of the above exercises is to drive home a point that when wrong is done, there is a way to make it right; however, simply wanting to make it right, doesn't correct the situation. There is something that must be done, an action which must be taken.

lesson summary

Up to this point in this book we have looked at sin entering the world, God's chosen people, and God's patience and love. In this lesson we are going to look at the ways God set up for the children of Israel to make right their wrongs.

text

We read toward the end of the book of Exodus where God describes in detail how the tabernacle, the place of sacrifice and worship, is to be built. Moses and the children of Israel build it to the exact measurements and description that God gives them.

After the book of Exodus, comes the book called Leviticus. Leviticus deals with the priestly tribe (Levites) and with the sacrifices and laws for the children of Israel. It is here we want to begin to look at what God's plan is under the old covenant to deal with sin.

Under the old covenant, the children of Israel were commanded to sacrifice animals or grain to God. There were certain places in the tabernacle that each sacrifice had to be made, and there was a certain order to making the sacrifice.

We are not commanded to make these types of sacrifices today; however, I want you to see that blood was shed to deal with sins even in the Old Testament.

5 Major Types of Sacrifices

1. Burnt Offering – (Leviticus 1: 3-17)
Purpose: to atone for unwitting sin in general
Now some of you may be wondering what "unwitting" means and what "atone" means. Sometimes it's best to define them before you can truly understand them.
"Unwitting" - sins of ignorance, or unplanned sins, or sins committed in a moment of weakness
"Atone" - sacrifice to remove the effects of sin; able to restore fellowship, relationship with God (Holman Concise Bible Dictionary)

2. Sin Offering – (Leviticus 4: 1-12)
Purpose: to atone for a specific unwitting sin

3. Guilt Offering – (Leviticus 5: 14-6:7)

Purpose: to atone for unwitting sin requiring restitution

This big phrase "requiring restitution" simply means they had to go back and fix or make right what they had done before coming and offering the sacrifice.

4. Grain Offering – (Leviticus 2: 1-16)

Purpose: to secure or to retain good standings with God

5. Peace Offering – (Leviticus 3: 1-17)

Purpose: to give thanks to God

This sacrifice had a "fellowship meal" nature to it. They would burn the fat portions. Then the priest would eat some of the meat, and those who had brought the sacrifice would eat the other portions.

There is a very interesting fact you need to know about these sacrifices. They had to be offered continually. Every time someone sinned, they had to go and offer a sacrifice. In Hebrews we read, "*they offered them continually year by year.*"

Hebrews 10:11: "*Every priest stands daily ministering and offering time after time the same sacrifices.*"

This sacrificial system was God's way of allowing the children of Israel to make atonement for their sins. However, this system was not perfect. We read in the book of Hebrews chapter 10 verses 1-4, "*For the Law, since it has only a shadow of the good things to come and not the very form of things, can never, by the same sacrifices which they offer continually year by year, make perfect those who draw near. Otherwise, would they not have ceased to be offered, because the worshipers, having once been cleansed, would no longer have consciousness of sins? But in those sacrifices there is a reminder of sins year by year. For it is impossible for the blood of bulls and goats to take away sins."*

There was something that had to happen in order to take away sins. We will get into this in the next chapters.

lessons learned

1) God had a plan to deal with sin.

In the Bible, we learn that doing wrong comes with consequence. God, in His love, would allow humans to offer sacrifices to atone for their sins. His plan in the Old Testament was the sacrificial system that involved the blood of bulls and goats.

2) The old system was not perfect.

This is a tough concept for everyone to understand, not just teens. The old system was not perfect, and there was to come a great sacrifice. This great sacrifice would do away with the old sacrificial system and would be far greater because of the Lamb that was to be offered and the strength and longevity of the sacrifice.

recap

Whether it involves stolen money, a "borrowed-without-returning" video game, or cheating on homework, wrong is wrong, regardless of the reasons. As a person who wants to follow God, you really only have one option– you must make it right. Fortunately, in the cases we looked at, there is a "right" response that involves what is called "restitution."

In our lesson, we learn that God provided a way in the Old Testament for His children to make right their wrongs. For them, it was about obedience to God, doing what He required of them in the sacrificial system. The "righting" of the wrong was accomplished by God, but it required the submission and obedience of the person. This old system was not perfect, and a better sacrifice came which would allow man the opportunity to deal with the sins in their lives once and for all.

questions for thought

1. Have you ever done anything in your life that required that you make "restitution" for it?

2. Think of an example of sacrifice in our day in time. Have you ever done anything that demanded sacrifice in your life?

3. Why is it a struggle for us to admit when we have done something wrong?

4. If you knew the true way that God provided for your sins to be "cleaned up" would you do that? Why? Why not?

chapter six:
the new is born

introduction

It was just like every other Saturday. The kids woke up earlier than their parents and went downstairs to eat a bowl of cereal while they watched their favorite cartoons. Seeing as how Saturday is the only morning they can sleep in, dad and mom slept in a little longer, but not too late because today was Yard Sale day! They were all going to stop at a few yard sales and see what junk they could get at a great price.

The first stop was not too far from their house. The kids got out of the car and rushed over to the goodies. As they started looking around, one of them, without knowing what it was, picked up an old tape player. After messing with it for a few minutes, trying to figure out its purpose, the boy asked, "Hey dad, what is this thing?" His father grinned as he took it from his son. "Buddy, this is a tape player," he replied. "A tape player?" his son asked. "What is a tape?" For the first time, his father realized that his boy was disconnected from his own childhood experiences. In a day of iPods and digital downloads, his boy had no idea what a tape was, nor did he understand the need for a tape player.

"Son, there was a time when we didn't have iPods or computers like you have today," his father began. "We had to stick this little rectangular thing called a 'tape' in the stereo and record the music from the radio," he continued. "Once we had the music on the tape, we then used one of these tape players to listen to it." With a puzzled look on his face, his son put the tape player down and walked away as he thought to himself, "Why would anyone buy that? Most people I know don't even have tapes anymore."

lesson summary

In this chapter we are going to talk about this very idea of something being out-of-date and replaced by something new and better. The birth of Jesus brought the fulfillment of prophecy, and His death brought the new covenant into being.

text

The most information about the birth of Christ is given in the Gospel according to Luke. In Luke 1:30-33, we read, *"The angel said to her, 'Do not be afraid, Mary; for you have found favor with God. And behold, you will conceive in your womb and bear a son, and you shall name Him Jesus. He will be great and will be called the Son of the Most High; and the Lord God will give Him the throne of His father David; and He will reign over the house of Jacob forever, and His kingdom will have no end."*

We then read in Luke 2:4-6 that Mary and Joseph were traveling to Bethlehem ("City of David") to register for the census that Caesar Augustus had demanded. While they were there, Jesus was born.

chapter 6: the new is born

An angel of the Lord appeared to shepherds, who were in the same region, and said, *"Do not be afraid; for behold, I bring you good news of great joy which will be for all the people; for today in the city of David there has been born for you a Savior, who is Christ the Lord."*

Notice the angel of the Lord told the shepherds a Savior was born. What does that word mean? The word *"Savior"* means: 1) "to make safe or free" or 2) *"Deliverer."* Jesus is the "Deliverer" who was born.

We can learn more about Jesus and where He came from by reading John 1:1, *"In the beginning was the Word, and the Word was with God, and the Word was God."*

We can also learn more about *"the Word"* by reading John 1:14, *"And the Word became flesh, and dwelt among us, and we saw His glory, glory as of the only begotten from the Father, full of grace and truth."*

The prophet Isaiah prophesied the coming of Jesus in the Old Testament. Now we need to understand the word *"prophesy"* before we continue.

"Prophesy" - to tell the past, present, or future

In Isaiah chapter 7 verse 14 we read, *"Therefore the Lord Himself will give you a sign: Behold, a virgin will be with child and bear a son, and she will call His name Immanuel."*

The name *"Immanuel"* means "God with us."

We know the birth of Jesus was prophesied, but why was Jesus to be born? The answer to this question was also prophesied about in the Old Testament by the prophet Jeremiah in chapter 31:31-33: *"Behold, days are coming', declares the Lord, 'when I will make a new covenant with the house of Israel and with the house of Judah, not like the covenant which I made with their father in the day I took them by the hand to bring them out of the land of Egypt, My covenant which they broke, although*

I was a husband to them,' declares the Lord. 'But this is the covenant which I will make with the house of Israel after those days.' declares the Lord. 'I will put My law within them and on their heart I will write it; and I will be their God, and they shall be My people."

Jesus came to this earth because God was going to establish a new covenant not like the old one. We read in Hebrews 9: 17-20, *"For a covenant is valid only when men are dead, for it is never in force while the one who made it lives. Therefore even the first covenant was not inaugurated without blood. For when every commandment had been spoken by Moses to all the people according to the Law, he took the blood of the calves and the goats, with water and scarlet wool and hyssop, and sprinkled both the book itself and all the people, saying, 'THIS IS THE BLOOD OF THE COVENANT WHICH GOD COMMANDED YOU."*

It was for this reason that Jesus came to this earth and went to the cross. God wanted to establish a new covenant with His people, and this was the way He did it. The death of Jesus brought about the New Covenant.

lessons learned

1) The birth of Jesus was prophesied in the Old Testament.

This is a very important lesson because it shows God's plan. He didn't just all of a sudden one day decide to start a new covenant. He had intended to do this long before the birth of Christ. He knew the Old Covenant was void because the children of Israel had broken it. God didn't leave though. He had a new covenant in mind.

2) The blood of Christ started the New Covenant.

When you decide you want to buy your first car, you are going to have to sign a contract. That contract will not be in effect until you sign your name. It is at that time it will become binding. You will be under that contract. The New Covenant is the same way. It did not come into effect until Jesus died on the cross. It is His blood, which is the signature that started it.

recap

There are many things your parents grew up using that are no longer needed. Items like the tape player from the yard sale may be cool, at least for some; however, with all the new and advanced technology there really isn't a good reason to keep it. The old is out, and the new is in. In the same way, as we study the Old Covenant and the New Covenant, the old is out and the new is in. That's God's design and is God's plan. You need to understand this point before moving forward. You are to learn what God desires under the New Covenant and follow that.

questions for thought

1. Have you ever noticed how things, that maybe at one time were needed can be replaced by newer items? What makes something no longer needed?

2. Have you ever had to sign a contract? What was it dealing with?

3. How did you feel after you signed and were under the terms of the contract?

4. Would you ever consider entering a "contract" with God? Why? Or Why not?

chapter seven:
the gospel is proclaimed

introduction

"It's so late, and he's just getting started," Eric thought to himself. "How is he ever going to finish in time?"

"How does she get her hair to stay in that position?" Eric contemplated as the preacher was getting through his first point. "I'm guessing she had to use at least a full can of hairspray, possibly a little hair gel as well."

"My eyes are getting so heavy. I can't keep them open any more," Eric thought as his head began to tilt down. "Is he ever going to finish?"

Have you ever thought about why people come to worship services to sit and listen to a preacher preach? What is it about that sermon that is important to our lives? A lot of times we sit there and let our minds wander. One lady told a story saying, "My young son asked what was the highest number I had ever counted to. I didn't know but asked about his highest number. It was "5,372."

"Oh," I said. "Why did you stop there?"

"Church was over."

We are like this boy sometimes when it comes to worship. As much as we might like to make everyone think we are paying attention all the time, the reality is, we aren't. We get distracted, and our minds begin to wander. It seems no matter what we do, we just can't focus. Our minds go everywhere except on the lesson. We sit there, but it might be that we don't fully appreciate the message being proclaimed. What if we actually listened to what the preacher was saying? Would his message possibly change our lives?

lesson summary

In this lesson we are going to study the first recorded Gospel sermon preached. We will look at what was preached and what the reaction was.

text

We begin our study in the book of Mark chapter 16 verse 15 when Jesus speaking to His 11 apostles said, *"Go into all the world and preach the gospel to all creation."*

What did He mean, *"preach the gospel"*? What is the gospel? That is a great question, and I am glad you asked. The gospel is the good news about Jesus and His death, burial, and resurrection. Jesus told them to go and preach this to the entire world. But why? Why preach the gospel? Well, let's put that question on hold for just a moment. We will come back to it.

After Jesus gives this command to the apostles, we can turn to the book of Acts, and find all the apostles gathered in one place. It is here that Jesus tells them, *" for John baptized with water, but you will be baptized with the Holy Spirit not many days from now."*

In the first verse of Acts chapter 2 we find that it is the day of Pentecost, which is a Jewish sacred day that occurs 50 days after the Passover. It is a celebration of the first fruits of the wheat harvest. Pentecost is a day when the Jews show joy and thankfulness for the Lord's blessings of harvest.

This piece of information is very important because we will find there are many Jews from every nation who gather in Jerusalem for this feast. It is these Jews who witnessed what is written in Acts 2:2-4: *"And suddenly there came from heaven a noise like a violent rushing wind, and it filled the whole house where they were sitting. And there appeared to them tongues as of fire distributing themselves, and they rested on each one of them. And they were all filled with the Holy Spirit and began to speak with other tongues, as the Spirit was giving them utterance."*

On this day of Pentecost we find the apostles, with the power of the Holy Spirit, begin to speak in tongues. This is the baptism of the Holy Spirit Jesus talked about in Acts 1:5. It is the Holy Spirit that allows them to speak in tongues, or different languages. (We know this because the text says that the Jews could understand them in their own languages.)

The Jews who are gathered there because of the day of Pentecost, each in his own native language, hear the apostles speaking of the mighty deeds of God (Acts 2: 11). This is very unusual because the apostles are not scholars. They are Galileans, fishermen, tax collectors, and such.

Some of the men begin to dismiss the apostles' teaching by saying they are filled with sweet wine (Acts 2:13). However, we find that Peter (yes, the one who had denied Jesus 3 times) stands up and takes his stand with the others. Peter tells the onlookers they are not drunk, and then he goes on to preach what is commonly known as the first gospel sermon we have recorded in writing.

Well, how does this sermon affect those Jews who heard? We read in Acts 2:37, *"Now when they heard this, they were pierced to the heart, and said to Peter and the rest of the apostles, 'Brethren, what shall we do?'"*

They are so convicted by what Peter had said, and wanted to know what to do. Peter tells them,

"Repent, and each of you be baptized in the name of Jesus Christ for the forgiveness of your sins; and you will receive the gift of the Holy Spirit." (Acts 2: 38)

lessons learned

1) The Gospel is the power.

Earlier in this chapter we asked the question, "Why preach the Gospel?" I want you to pay special attention to this next verse, which is the answer. *"For I am not ashamed of the gospel, for it is the power of God for salvation to everyone who believes, to the Jew first and also to the Greek"* (Rom. 1:16).

A man who stands up on Sunday morning needs to preach the Gospel just like Peter did, because as Paul writes in Rom. 1:16, that is where the power is.

2) What should we do with the Gospel?

Have you ever heard someone say something that really got you thinking about your life and where you are heading? Have you ever heard something that made you feel weird inside, and you knew you needed to change? If you are a normal teenager then the answer is more than likely yes. We have all heard something that made us feel this way, but the one thing that separates you from the group is what you do with that "gut feeling." On the day of Pentecost, we find those who heard it were *"pierced to their hearts."* Approximately 3,000 responded the way Peter told them to. The question to you is this: when you know you need to make a change, how do you handle it? How should you handle it?

recap

Have you ever had the opportunity to get something great, only you passed it up because you didn't fully understand the value it had? That's what it's like to "go to church" and not fully listen and hear the sermon. When the Word of God is preached, you have the tremendous opportunity to grow in your spiritual walk. If you will allow the Truth to take root in your life, you will never regret it.

questions for thought

1. Have you ever truly listened to a sermon? What's the difference between enduring a sermon and listening to a sermon?
2. What was your reaction to it after hearing it?
3. Have you ever been challenged by a sermon? How did you respond?
4. If you were a Jew on the day of Pentecost, and you heard Peter's sermon, what would you have done? Why?

chapter eight:
new testament conversions

introduction

Thirty-two degrees: that's what their teacher had always taught them was the magical number the temperature had to hit before snow could be a possibility. As their anticipation grew, they continually ran to check the weather app, hoping the forecast of snow was increasing. When it finally hit 32 degrees, their smiles grew as they thought, "Maybe these big clouds will begin to drop snow, and we can go outside and build a snowman!"

Fighting the urge to stand at the window forever, the children decided to sit down and watch a movie together. Before too long, one of them looked out the window and noticed it was raining. Rushing to the window, they all looked out with disappointment. "I thought it was supposed to snow when it hit 32 degrees," one of the boys said. "That's what we all thought," replied one of the girls. With disappointment written all over their faces, they returned to their movie trying to accept that snow wasn't going to happen today.

As the movie ended, one of the boys asked, "What should we do now?" All of a sudden, one of the girls yelled out, "SNOW!" With a quick bounce and leap, all the children rushed to a window to not only see snow falling, but the ground that was once wet, freezing with ice. In the time it took the movie to end, the temperature had continued to drop below 32 degrees, and the colder it got, the more it caused the rain to change into snow and ice.

"I guess our teacher was right," one of the girls said. "Yep. I guess it just took a little longer for the rain to change over," replied one of the guys.

lesson summary

In this lesson, we are going to study two cases of New Testament conversions in the Bible. As you grow in your understanding, you will see what each of these individuals did in their conversion.

text

Case 1:

After the day of Pentecost we find that the good news about Jesus spreads. Peter and the other apostles go everywhere preaching about Jesus and performing miracles in His name. Many are saved through baptism, and the church is growing.

We then find that there comes some persecutions against the church. We read of a man by the name of Saul (Acts 8) who goes into houses and drags out men and women and puts them in prison. Because of this persecution, the Christians flee Jerusalem and scatter out.

It is during this time that we meet another man by the name of Philip. Philip is a disciple who is busy preaching and teaching. On the way back from Samaria, an angel of the Lord (Acts 8:26) speaks to Philip and tells him to go south to Gaza.

There Philip sees an Ethiopian eunuch reading from the prophet Isaiah (chapter 53). The Spirit told Philip, *"Go up and join this chariot"* (Acts 8:29). Philip runs up to the chariot and hears the eunuch reading, and asks, *"Do you understand what you are reading?"* (Acts 8: 30). The eunuch then responds, *"Well, how could I, unless someone guides me?"* (Acts 8: 31)

It is at this point the eunuch lets Philip up into the chariot. Philip then, beginning in Isaiah, proceeds to preach Jesus to him. The Bible then tells us they came to some water and the eunuch said, *"Look! Water! What prevents me from being baptized?"* (Acts 8:36).

We find Philip reply, *"If you believe with all your heart, you may"* (Acts 8:37).

After the Ethiopian eunuch gives the good confession saying he believes Jesus Christ is the Son of God, the Bible tells us in verse 38 and 39, *"And he ordered the chariot to stop; and they both went down into the water, Philip as well as the eunuch, and he baptized him. When they came up out of the water, the Spirit of the Lord snatched Philip away;"*

Case 2:

Another New Testament conversion takes place in Acts chapter 16 verses 25-33. This is the account of the Philippian jailor. Paul and Silas have just cast out a demon from a slave-girl who was a fortuneteller. Her masters, after seeing they will no longer make money from her, are angry with Paul and Silas and drag them before the authorities. As a result of this event, Paul and Silas are thrown into prison and placed in the inner most part of the prison.

We read in Acts 16: 25, *"Paul and Silas were praying and singing hymns of praise to God, and the prisoners were listening to them"*.

About midnight, an earthquake occurs which shakes the prison doors open, and it shakes loose all the chains, which bind the prisoners. The jailor wakes up and sees what had happened, so he draws his sword to kill himself. To you and to me, this may sound like an extreme reaction from the jailor; however, it was a rule that he was to be put to death if the prisoners escaped. He was going to go ahead and do it.

We see Paul speak up and convince the jailor not to kill himself because all the prisoners were still there. This makes you think about the purpose of the earthquake. If it was to free Paul and Silas, they would have left and let the jailor kill himself; however, they didn't. Maybe there was a bigger picture to consider that involves the jailor's family. We see in Acts 16:30, 31 what the jailor asks Paul and Silas, and we can see their response.

"Sirs, what must I do to be saved?" (Acts 16:30)

"Believe in the Lord Jesus, and you will be saved, you and your household." (Acts 16:31)

We go on to read about Paul and Silas preaching to the jailor and his household, and the result after they studied is recorded in verse 33.

Before I leave this point, you need to understand something. When Paul and Silas said that if the jailor believed in the Lord Jesus he would be saved, they were not saying that baptism is not necessary. If it is not necessary, then why were the jailor and his family baptized after studying? One very important point to realize is that someone is not going to obey what is said if they do not believe first. Baptism is essential for salvation.

"Corresponding to that, baptism now saves you - not the removal of dirt from the flesh, but an appeal to God for a good conscience - through the resurrection of Jesus Christ" (1 Peter 3: 21).

lessons learned

1) There is a conversion that takes place.

In 2 Corinthians 5:17, we are told if anyone is in Christ then he is a new creature. In order to belong to Christ one must be converted or changed to a new creature.

2) The conversion happens when we obey the Gospel.

Baptism takes place in both cases in this chapter. We will see in the next two chapters of other instances of conversions, and you will see that baptism was a part of it as well.

recap

Conversion is an interesting subject. It doesn't matter if we're talking about water that is wet changing to water in the form of ice or snow, or if we're talking about someone leaving a life of sin and having their sins washed away. The subject of being converted, especially when we're talking about our life and walk with Jesus, is a serious subject and one that each of us needs to consider.

questions for thought

1. What caused the people we talked about to be baptized?
2. What drives people today, who hear the Gospel preached, to be baptized?
3. What keeps some away from being baptized?
4. If you have never been baptized, what is holding you back?

chapter nine: saul's conversion

introduction

This was not the plan. Leslie had been training for a long time for the scholastic challenge, and now she was laying in bed, sick as a dog. As her stomach ached, she thought to herself, "This is just not fair. Here I've been working so hard, and now I'm going to be passed over because of a stomach bug." Beginning to cry, she laid her head down on her pillow and turned towards the wall. "Why me?" she thought to herself. "This is not what I had planned."

Have you ever found yourself having to go a different direction other than the one you thought you'd go? Leslie's not the only one to miss a very important event in life because of sickness. Chances are you have been in her shoes before, and she's right – it isn't fair, but it's reality. Our plans and the direction we thought we would be taking aren't always the way things turn out.

In order to make it through this life, we must understand this point. It's not wrong to plan. As a matter of fact, God in His Word tells us it's wise to count the cost; that involves planning (Luke 14:28). However, we must accept that every plan we come up with isn't necessarily going to happen. Not every kid who plans to play professional football accomplishes that plan. For every young lady who plans to live in a big house with all the rooms perfectly decorated, there are plenty of failed dreams as life doesn't always present ways and opportunities to achieve such plans.

Planning is good, but planning and leaving room for God's will is better. What if your plans aren't His plans? Would you really want them to work out anyway? What if your plans end up taking you down a path of hurt and pain? Would you really want those plans to work out? Sometimes, the direction we see ourselves taking is not really the direction we need to take. That's where we see a man named Saul in our lesson today.

lesson summary

In today's lesson, we are going to look at this man Saul. He had much training in a certain area. He had planned to live a certain way; however, the Lord had a different plan for Saul.

text

In Acts 7:58 through chapter 8:4, we read the account where the disciple Stephen is stoned to death by the Pharisees. Here we read the Council had gotten so enraged with Stephen they drove him out of the city, and there they stoned him. An interesting point to note is the place where the men laid their coats. The Bible says in chapter 7:58b, *"And the witnesses laid aside their robes at the feet of a young man named Saul."*

This is the first time in the New Testament we are introduced to Saul. We find Saul on the side of the Pharisees, in agreement with the stoning of Stephen (Acts 8:1). Let's take a closer look at who this man was.

Saul was from the tribe of Benjamin (Phil 3: 5). He was born in Tarsus (Acts 22:3) around the same time as Jesus. His father was a Pharisee (Acts 23:6), and his mother was a Jew (Gal. 1:15). Saul had relatives just like you and I. He also had at least one sister (Acts 23:16) and a nephew who later helped save his life (Acts 23:12-24).

Saul was highly educated in the old Law. He went to a "rabbi's school" where he studied at the feet of Gamaliel (Acts 22:3), an honor to say the least. The students didn't play at these schools. The instructor would recite the Torah, and the students would then repeat it. Now, I don't know about you, but if my teachers had tried to teach me that way I think I would have gone to sleep.

Now, Saul also mentions in Acts 22:3 he was born in Tarsus of Cilicia, which was a province of Rome. He was a Roman citizen, which comes into play when Paul is imprisoned or on trial. Let's get back to the stoning of Stephen.

Saul is there holding the coats and in agreement with what they were doing. How do you think this man was feeling? What could have possibly been going on in his mind? Well, let's let Paul's answer. In I Timothy chapter 1 verses 12 and 13 we read, *"I thank Christ Jesus our Lord, who has strengthened me, because He considered me faithful, putting me into service, even though I was formerly a blasphemer and a persecutor and a violent aggressor."*

We find this man persecuting the church in Acts chapter 8 by going into houses and dragging out men and women and putting them into prison. He thought he was doing what he was supposed to do. He really thought he was making God happy by doing this. After all, these Christians were saying the old Law was done away with and a new covenant was here.

As Saul was on his way to Damascus to persecute those of the Way (Acts 9), we find a very interesting thing happen to Saul. We read in the later part of Acts 9:3 and following, *"and suddenly a light from heaven flashed around him; and he fell to the ground and heard a voice saying to him, 'Saul, Saul, why are you persecuting Me?' And he said, 'Who are you, Lord?' And He said, 'I am Jesus whom you are persecuting, but get up and enter the city, and it will be told you what you must do.'"*

Saul went into Damascus and stayed there for three days without eating or drinking anything. The Lord then brings a man named Ananias to Saul and commands him to touch Saul so he could regain his sight. Ananias was scared, which is understandable, but God told him he must go. In Acts 9:15, we read, *"Go, for he is a chosen instrument of Mine, to bear My name before the Gentiles and kings and the sons of Israel; for I will show him how much he must suffer for My name's sake."*

God had a purpose for Saul. He was going to use Saul to preach to the Gentiles, kings, and the sons of Israel. Now before we go on, I want to make sure you understand what a Gentile is. A Gentile is simply anyone who was not born a Jew. The sons of Israel were Jews, and everyone else was a Gentile. Saul was to preach and teach **everyone**.

We know that Saul had been in Damascus for three days before Ananias came to him. We know that he had been praying, but eating and not drinking. We also see in vs. 18 that Saul still obeys the gospel, *"And immediately there fell from his eyes something like scales, and he regained his sight, and he got up and was baptized."*

Chapter 9: Saul's Conversion

Paul retells this same account later in the book of Acts. In chapter 22 and verse 16 Paul reports that Ananias said, *"Now why do you delay? Get up and be baptized, and wash away your sins, calling on His name."*

Paul spent the rest of his life preaching the gospel of Jesus Christ, and wrote almost half of the New Testament by the inspiration of the Holy Spirit. Not only was he a great man in the 1st century church, but his whole life was planned out. He was to have it all; however, God saw Paul in a another way, and had a different plan for him.

lessons learned

1) Paul planned his steps, but God directed them.

In Proverbs 16: 9 we are told, *"The mind of man plans his way, but the Lord directs his steps."* We can make plans all day long, but just remember that it is God who will direct our steps. Be useful where ever He directs you.

2) Saul still had to be baptized.

Some religions want to teach that all you have to do is believe and say the "sinner's prayer" to be saved. Saul had spent three days in fasting and prayer, and he still was baptized to wash away his sins. It was at this time that he was saved.

recap

Sometimes our plans change. The direction we plan our lives taking doesn't always come to be. For Saul, as he sat at the feet of the great Jewish teacher, he wasn't thinking of leaving Judaism. He wasn't thinking about obeying the Gospel in baptism. We know this because his life was demonstrating his plan. As you think about this lesson today, can it be said of you that your plan involves walking with Jesus? If so, you have to be willing to possibly alter your other plans so this one big plan can be first.

questions for thought

1. What are some of the plans that you have right now?
2. What are some of the things that change when you are baptized and become a Christian?
3. Paul had to be baptized to wash away his sins. Do you think that you also must be baptized to wash away your sins?
4. In 2 Peter 3:9 we find that God doesn't want any to perish, but all to come to repentance. On a separate piece of paper, write the one major thing that is keeping you from becoming a Christian.

chapter ten:
cornelius' conversion

introduction

Walking through the halls of his new school was pretty intimidating. Joe had just moved from a place where everyone wore really nice, name brand clothes to another school where most people didn't seem to care about any of that. Upon entering his new homeroom, he couldn't help but notice the eyes of the rest of the teens staring directly at him. They all knew he wasn't from there. They had never seen Joe before in their lives. It was one of the loneliest feelings Joe had ever experienced.

The bell sounded to release the kids from homeroom and send them to first period. As Joe walked out the door, one of the boys bumped him. Looking back grinning he said, "Oh sorry 'new kid.' I didn't see you there." Wishing he could simply blend into the walls and go unnoticed, Joe walked on talking to no one. After first period, a few girls came up and began talking to him. "What's your name?" one asked. "Where are you from?" said another. Joe politely answered them and the girls began to giggle. "We love your accent," they said as they asked him to say something else. Joe, enjoying the friendliness, began to let his guard down. As they walked with him to the next class, he relaxed a little. Even though he wasn't "one of them" he thought, maybe he was still going to be able to make friends and adjust.

As the day came to an end, and Joe got home, his mother greeted him, "How was your day?" Tired from his first full day Joe sat down and said, "It was okay. It started off rough and I felt like I wasn't accepted because I am not from here, but then as the day continued, people started talking to me and treating me better." His mother hugged him, and assuredly sat homemade cookies on the table. "You don't need to change to become one of them sweetheart. God loves you and has made you just the way you are. They will see that and, in time, accept you," his mother wisely counseled.

lesson summary

In chapter three, we discussed how the Jews were God's chosen people. It was the children of Israel that God preserved. It was understood by the Jews that God was only for them. We are going to see in this chapter that God was not just for the Jews, but He was also for the Gentiles.

text

In the last chapter we established what a Gentile was, but just in case you forgot, a Gentile is simply anyone who is not born a Jew. We are all Gentiles (that is, unless you were born a Jew). Our study begins in Acts chapter 10 verses 1-8, where we learn of a man by the name of Cornelius.

Chapter 10: Cornelius' Conversion

Cornelius was from Caesarea. He was a centurion of the Italian cohort, so we know that he was an army officer. The Bible describes him as a *"devout man (heartfelt or sincere), one who feared God with all his household,"* (Acts 10:2). We know he was a generous man, because he gave alms (or money) to the poor Jewish people. We also know Cornelius talked to God regularly through prayer.

The Bible tells us that Cornelius had a vision. He saw an angel of God who had just come in and the Bible says, *"Cornelius!' And fixing his gaze on him and being much alarmed, he said, 'What is it Lord?' And he said to him, 'Your prayers and alms have ascended as a memorial before God. Now dispatch some men to Joppa and send for a man named Simon, who is also called Peter, he is staying with a tanner named Simon, who house is by the sea"* (Acts 10: 3-6).

Cornelius did as he was told, and we then turn our attention to Joppa where the apostle Peter is, just as the angel of the Lord had said. He has gone up on the roof of the building where he is staying to pray. He becomes hungry, and while he waits on the food to be prepared the Bible says, *"He fell into a trance; and he saw the sky opened up, and an object like a great sheet coming down, lowered by four corners to the ground, and there were in it all kinds of four-footed animals and crawling creatures on the earth and birds of the air"* (Acts 10:10-12).

A voice comes to Peter, *"Get up, Peter, kill and eat!"* (Acts 10:13).

He hears the voice, but isn't really sure that he can do as was commanded. Peter replied, *"By no means, Lord, for I have never eaten anything unholy and unclean."* (Acts 10:14).

Now, Peter is not talking about a dirty food like you and I would think. He is talking about an animal that according to the Jewish custom would be considered unclean. In the Jewish religion, there are some animals that are unclean due to physical features or other varies reasons, not because they have dirt on them. It is important to understand that Peter is thinking in the ways of his Jewish background.

The voice then spoke to Peter again saying, *"What God has cleansed, no longer consider unholy"* (Acts 10: 15).

The Bible then goes on to tell us that this happens three times, then the object is immediately taken up. Peter wakes up but does not understand this. As he is thinking about the dream, Cornelius' men come to him and tell him he must come with them to the house of Cornelius. Peter goes without questioning them.

The Bible tells us that as soon as Peter comes to the house, Cornelius falls at his feet. Peter tells him to get up and says something that is so important: *"You yourselves know how unlawful it is for a man who is a Jew to associate with a foreigner or to visit him; and yet God has shown me that I should not call any man unholy or unclean"* (Acts 10:28).

Cornelius begins to tell Peter about the vision he had. It is at this point that Peter begins to open his eyes. It is like when you have had a really tough time understanding a math problem, and all of a sudden it makes sense to you. This is what was going on with Peter. Peter says in Acts 10:34, *"I most certainly understand now that God is not one to show partiality, but in every nation the man who fears Him and does what is right is welcome to Him."*

This is one of the biggest events that takes place in the New Testament. Up until this point, it was thought that God was only for the Jews, and now it has changed. God is for the Gentiles too.

Chapter 10: Cornelius' Conversion

Peter begins to preach to Cornelius and the rest of the Gentiles, and the Bible tells us, *"While Peter was still speaking these words, the Holy Spirit fell upon all those who were listening to the message"* (Acts 10:44). All the circumcised believers who were with Peter were amazed. They were hearing the Gentiles speak in tongues. The Holy Spirit had been given to the Gentiles to prove to the Jews that God was for everyone. It was at this point that Peter said, *"Surely no one can refuse the water for these to be baptized who have received the Holy Spirit just as we did can he?"* (Acts 10:47). We read that Peter ordered all the Gentiles, who were gathered, to be baptized in the name of Jesus Christ.

lessons learned

1) Jesus died for everyone.

This was a foreign concept for Peter and the other Jews up to this point. However, God had a bigger plan than just the Jews. His plan included everyone, and that means you and me.

2) The Gentiles were still baptized.

Some people would like to believe that since the Gentiles here received the Holy Spirit before baptism they were then saved. Notice though that Peter still baptized them. The Holy Spirit that came on them gave them miraculous gifts to prove to Peter and the others that God was for everyone. The Gentiles were still baptized. Acts chapter two and verse 38 is still true.

recap

Sometimes it's hard being the new kid in school, especially when it seems everyone has grown up together and you're the outsider. You may be tempted to change to fit in; however, that's not the best plan. In our lesson today, we learned that God is not just the God of the Jews. The Gentiles were the outsiders as far as the Jews were concerned, but God shows everyone that His love reaches even those some may consider the outsiders.

questions for thought

1. Have you ever been an "outsider"? If so, how did it make you feel?
2. How would your life be different if Jesus had not died for all?
3. Does it really mean anything to you to know that Jesus did, in fact, die for you?
4. What is keeping you from being obedient to God's Word?

chapter eleven:
what must i do to be saved?

introduction

"What did she say?" Sarah asked regarding the instructions of the teacher. "She said if we wanted to get a homework pass, we have to win the math contest," Julie replied. "Homework pass? I guess she means if we are the winners today, then we will get a pass to use whenever we want." Sarah continued. "That's right! All you have to do is be the last person standing. Of course, that's not going to happen because I'm going to win, so you won't have to worry about it," Julie bragged. "We'll see about that," Sarah thought to herself.

"Alright students. Line up in two lines in the middle of the classroom," the teacher instructed. The first two students in the lines looked intently at the teacher, awaiting the math problem. As the teacher held up a card with an equation on it, the students rushed to the white board and began hurriedly working out the problem. One by one, there was a winner and a loser of each round. The student who lost had to sit down. The one that would win, continued to the back of the line to face another opponent. Finally, there were just two left.

"I told you I was going to win and that you wouldn't have to worry about the homework pass," Julie said trying to intimidate Sarah. She just ignored her and waited, anticipating the flip of the card. All of a sudden, the card flipped and Sarah rushed to the board. Her mind was going so fast that she was already a step ahead in solving the problem before she ever began writing the equation on the board. Julie also took off running for the board and got there about the same time. Both girls rushed to complete the math problem as fast as they could.

"Done!" Sarah yelled as she put her marker down on the ledge. The teacher looked Sarah's work over and announced, "Sarah's the winner!" She went over to her desk and handed Sarah the homework pass that read: "This Homework Pass is Good for One Free Night of Homework." Sarah was so proud she had been able to do just as the teacher said. She had paid attention when the teacher taught each lesson, and now it has finally paid off. Because she had listened, learned, and done what was required, she was able to cherish her reward.

lesson summary

Your salvation is much the same as the above story. Many people will tell you what you must do to be saved; however, many times they will overstep the limits and tell you what they think. Is there a better way to find out what you really have to do to be saved? You better believe there is. LET THE WORD OF GOD TELL YOU. It is that simple. Don't cut anything out, and leave everything in. That is what we are going to do in this chapter. Let God answer this question of "What Must I Do to Be Saved?".

text

In the past three chapters we have looked at some conversions that took place in the Bible. There is nothing that we have added. We have simply listened to the Word of God. Consider this journey to salvation.

Hear

"*So faith comes from hearing, and hearing by the word of Christ*" (Romans 10:17).

"*Philip went down to the city of Samaria and began proclaiming Christ to them. The crowds with one accord were giving attention to what was said by Philip, as they heard and saw the signs which he was performing*" (Acts 8:5-6).

Hear what? We are to hear the gospel or good news of Jesus Christ. He was born of a virgin, He went to the cross for you and for me, and He was raised from the dead on the third day. It is because of this that we have a hope of being able to be saved.

Believe

"*Therefore I said to you that you will die in your sins; for unless you believe that I am He, you will die in your sins*" (John 8:24).

"*And without faith it is impossible to please Him, for he who comes to God must believe that He is and that He is a rewarder of those who seek Him*" (Hebrews 11:6).

There is a misunderstanding by many in thinking this is the last step for salvation. Some would have us believe all you have to do is believe. Read these next verses.

"He who believes in the Son has eternal life; but he who does not obey the Son will not see life, but the wrath of God abides on him" (John 3:36).

Here the words "*believe*" and "*obey*" are used to mean the same thing. If one believes then they have eternal life. The next part of the verse says he who does not obey will not see life, or it could say if you obey then you will see life. The point is believing and obeying go hand-in-hand. Salvation does not stop with belief.

Repent

"*I tell you, no, but unless you repent, you will all likewise perish*" (Luke 13:3).

"*Therefore having overlooked the times of ignorance, God is now declaring to men that all people everywhere should repent*" (Acts 17:30).

What is true repentance? The simple definition of repentance is to change one's mind. We must change our mind about living a way that is not in the footsteps of Jesus. When we change our minds, our actions will also change. True repentance must take place.

"*You cannot drink the cup of the Lord and the cup of demons; you cannot partake of the table of the Lord and the table of demons*" (I Corinthians 10:21).

Confess

"*Therefore everyone who confesses Me before men, I will also confess him before My Father who is in heaven*" (Matthew 10:32).

Jesus asked the apostles, "*Who do you say that I am?*" (Matthew 16:15).

Peter replied, "*You are the Christ, the Son of the living God.*" (Matthew 16:16).

This is our biblical example of the "Great Confession." Like the Ethiopian eunuch in Acts 8:37, we must all make this good confession.

"...that if you confess with you mouth Jesus as Lord, and believe in your heart that God raised Him from the dead, you will be saved; for with the heart a person believes, resulting in righteousness, and with the mouth he confesses, resulting in salvation" (Romans 10:9-10).

The interesting thing about this particular text is how it leaves the impression with many in the religious world that all you have to do is verbally say "Jesus is Lord," and you'll be saved. Remember, Romans chapter 10 comes after Romans chapter 1-9. Up to this point, Paul has been telling them of the importance of being in the right slave/master relationship. In chapter 6, he tells them they will either be a slave of righteousness or a slave of sin. The difference is which one the person is chained or shackled to. When a person is baptized, he or she becomes shackled to righteousness. Therefore, if one is a Christian and confesses Jesus as Lord, he or she has actually made him Lord of his or her life by being submissive and obedient. Just remember, the teaching in Romans chapter 10 comes after all the teaching in chapters 1-9; you can't confess without being submissive and obedient.

Baptism

"Peter said to them, 'Repent, and each of you be baptized in the name of Jesus Christ for the forgiveness of your sins; and you will receive the gift of the Holy Spirit" (Acts 2:38).

"He who has believed and has been baptized shall be saved; but he who has disbelieved shall be condemned" (Mark 16:16).

In every example that we read in the New Testament, we find baptism is a part of salvation. We see it with the believers on the Day of Pentecost, with the Ethiopian eunuch, the Philippian jailor, with Saul, and with Cornelius. Our biblical example is that a person is saved after baptism.

"Corresponding to that, baptism now saves you - not the removal of dirt from the flesh, but an appeal to God for a good conscience - through the resurrection of Jesus Christ" (1 Peter 3:21).

lessons learned

1) God wants to forgive you of your sins.

It may sound funny, but God wants to forgive you of your sins more than you want to be forgiven of your sins. The Bible teaches us that He does not want anyone to perish as a result of their sins (2 Peter 3:9). He wants you to spend eternity with Him in heaven forever.

2) God has provided a plan of salvation.

While many people will tell you what they think needs to happen to receive salvation, the truth is, you need to listen to God's Word more than you need to listen to everyone else. Grace is God's to give, and He gives this wonderful, free gift through His Son. Therefore, if you want to be forgiven of your sins, you must follow the plan God has outlined.

Chapter 11: what must i do to be saved?

recap

There is a great reward for those who obey Jesus Christ (Hebrews 5:9). This reward is called *"salvation,"* and it is promised for all those who follow the instructions as God has outlined in the Bible. Like Sarah, we must listen, and learn, and do what God has instructed us. In so doing, we will be qualified by God for salvation, because He has told us we will receive the forgiveness of our sins.

questions for thought

1. Write on a piece of paper some things that are right in God's eyes and some that are wrong.
2. Have you reached the stage in life where you know the difference between right and wrong?
3. Are there sins in your life?
4. Are you ready to have those sins erased?
5. What does it mean to make a commitment to follow God?

chapter twelve:
now that i'm saved, what's next?

introduction

She is bound and determined to be different. Now that Erin is a Christian, things have to change, even if her friends don't understand it. Her commitment to Christ means more to her than her acceptance amongst the other teens, and she is determined to begin anew, starting with today.

"Erin, did you hear what Katie said about Jessica?" Haley asks as the two girls walk to their locker. Typically, Erin would have chimed right back in a way that begged for the gossip and detail; however, this time she stops herself, realizing she could no longer respond in the same manner. "I have not heard what Katie said, but I do not want to know", she says lovingly to Haley. "I was baptized Sunday, and I'm trying to not get wrapped up in talking about people", Erin continues to explain.

As the week progressed, Erin finds herself thinking a lot more about her actions, her dress, her behavior, and even her friends. "Erin, why have you changed so much? What's going on?" her friend, Laura, asks. "Laura, this past Sunday, I obeyed the Gospel. I repented of my sins and was baptized so my sins would be washed away", Erin explains. "Now that I'm a disciple of Jesus Christ, my life is not going to be the same as it once was", she continues. "So you're changed?" Laura asked a little confused. "That's right, and I'd love the opportunity to tell you why I've changed", Erin excitedly offered because Laura was showing interest in her new life in Christ.

This illustration may sound too simple, but it drives home a point. That point is that when someone obeys the Gospel, they are to be forever different. That difference shows in the way they walk and talk. It also shows in the friends they hang out with and even in their activities. They want to be more involved with the Church, and they are excited at every opportunity they have to worship God. In short, their perspective on life is different because they are different. It's this difference that comes about after their conversion. They are to put to death the old way of doing things (this was when they were living for themselves), and they are to put on what the Bible calls the "new self" (Ephesians 4:24).

lesson summary

In this chapter we are going to focus on two things: 1) What am I to do now? and 2) What about other people?

text

1) What am I to do now?

On the day of Pentecost there are about 3,000 people who are baptized and added to the church (Acts 2:41). In verse 42 we can read, *"They were continually devoting themselves to the apostles' teaching and to fellowship, to the breaking of bread and to prayer."*

The Bible says that those who believed were:

1) Devoting themselves to the apostles' teachings.

When we are baptized, we don't know everything about God, the Bible, or Christianity. We might know some, but we are babies in Christ. It is very important for all Christians, new or old, to continue studying the Word of God; however, there is more than just knowing the Bible. We must also live what the Bible says.

Peter and some of the other apostles were arrested for teaching the gospel of Jesus Christ. When they were challenged by the Council in Jerusalem to stop, Peter replied, *"We must obey God rather than men* (Acts 5:29)."

They knew what God said to do was much more important than what the Council told them to do. We must follow God before we follow men. In I John 1: 7, we read, *"but if we walk in the Light as He Himself is in the Light, we have fellowship with one another, and the blood of Jesus His Son cleanses us from all sin."*

There is a way a Christian must live. You may have to give up some of your favorite things. Your taste in music might have to change, you may need to stop watching your favorite TV shows, your Internet habits might need altered, and whatever else it takes to make sure you are living the Christian life God wants for you.

2) Devoting themselves to fellowship with one another.

People will influence us positively or negatively. Those you hang out with do have an impact on you. If you continually surround yourself with teens doing things that are not right, then it will rub off on you.

"*Do not be deceived: Bad company corrupts good morals*" (1 Corinthians 15: 33).

Spend more time with Christian teens. They will have the same goal as you: getting to heaven.

"*and let us consider how to stimulate one another to love and good deeds, not forsaking our own assembling together, as is the habit of some, but encouraging on another; and all the more as you see the day drawing near*" (Hebrews 10:24-25).

There are good reasons to come to worship: first and foremost to worship God the way He wants, secondly, to grow in knowledge of His Word, and thirdly, there is an element of being around other Christians that is good for you. It will encourage you, and you will gain strength from their friendships.

3) Devoting themselves to the breaking of bread and prayer.

We can read about the early Church and when they observed the breaking of bread, or Lord's Supper, in Acts 20:7, "*On the first day of the week, when we were gathered together to break bread, Paul began talking to them, intending to leave the next day, and he prolonged his message until midnight.*"

We, as New Testament Christians, must observe the Lord's Supper on the first day of the week. We also must continually pray to God. When we pray, we recognize we are not in control and that we need God's help. It is an awesome thing to be able to pray to God and know that we are in His hands. It makes life a lot easier to handle.

2) What about other people?

As teens, it is easy to get sidetracked with school, sports, or whatever else we value. We become so wrapped up in our lives that we forget that there is someone else out there too. There is something else a teenage Christian is supposed to do. Jesus Himself laid a charge out for all of us, *"Go therefore and make disciples of all the nations, baptizing them in the name of the Father and the Son and the Holy Spirit, teaching them to observe all that I commanded you; and lo, I am with you always, even to the end of the age"* (Matt. 28:19, 20).

This passage is said to the apostles; however, there is a message for all of us. We must be aware that our friends who are not forgiven of their sins are lost. You might say, "I don't want to believe that." I know that none of us like to think of our friends as being lost; however, 2 Thessalonians 1:8 makes it clear when it speaks of God, *"dealing out retribution to those who do not know God and to those who do not obey the gospel of our Lord Jesus."*

Talk to them and let them know there is something better, and Jesus has it.

lessons learned

1) The example in the Bible is one of devotion and change.

The early Church left so much when they converted out of Judaism and into a covenant relationship with Christ through repentance and baptism for the remission of their sins. This change not only included their submission to Christ but also in the way they worshipped and the need to build each other up in spending time together.

2) We must love our friends enough to tell them about Jesus.

When our lives have been changed by the blood of Jesus, we can't help but tell others what happened. We never really know how they will respond to our message, or even if they will be open to listening to us. However they may respond, you know they need the forgiveness of sins just as much as you do.

recap

Obeying the Gospel means so much more than simply "checking-off" a box on a "to-do list." There is a real change that occurs in the life of a new Christian. Like Erin in our opening illustration, when you are saved from the punishment of your sins, you will begin to think and act differently. This change will cause you to want to tell others of the great difference Jesus has made in your life. Love your friends enough to invite them to worship with you. Take the time to talk with them about their soul and their need for Jesus.

questions for thought

1. Do you know anyone who has not obeyed the Gospel of Jesus Christ?
2. Have you talked to them about it? Why or Why not?
3. Are you willing to give up things that will get in the way of you living the Christian life?
4. Do you think it is necessary for you to gather with other Christians and worship? Why or Why not?

chapter thirteen:
what will that day be like?

introduction

Imagine yourself in a courtroom, standing before the judge. The prosecuting attorney gets up and begins to lay out all the facts in the case against you. You begin to turn red in embarrassment as more and more is said. You have no defense, at least none that holds any weight. You can't defend your actions, thoughts, motives, or words. You know it and so does everyone else – you're guilty as charged.

Now your attorney begins. He looks at the judge and simply says, "Your Honor, everything the prosecutor has said is absolutely true. My client did all those things, thought in all those ways, and spoke every word." You sink even further and further inside of yourself. "But…" your attorney interjects. "Your Honor, he's been forgiven of all these trespasses. The arguments against him are no longer valid, and they hold no weight," your attorney boldly proclaims. "Father, he's one of Ours. He obeyed Your Word and because of faithful obedience, he was baptized for the forgiveness of sins. Father, he's forgiven," your attorney says as He looks lovingly in your direction.

If this was your trial today, and these events occurred, how would you feel at this moment? To go from knowing you were guilty to being absolutely forgiven and free because of who's side you were on would have to be one of the best feelings you could ever imagine.

To go from total guilt to total freedom— that's what this entire book has been about. We've considered how sin entered the world, and we've learned how God has dealt with sin throughout both the Old and the New Testaments. In this last chapter, we are going to study about this last great trial. Consider how your case would turn out if you had to stand before the Judge today.

lesson summary

In this last chapter we are going to look at the Judgment Day. It is not my intention to scare you; however, you do need to look at what the Bible says about that day.

text

To begin this chapter we are going to look at 2 Thessalonians chapter 4 verses 13-17.

"But we do not want you to be uninformed, brethren, about those who are asleep, so that you will not grieve as do the rest who have no hope. For if we believe that Jesus died and rose again, even so God will bring with Him those who are fallen asleep in Jesus. For this we say to you by the word of the Lord, that we who are alive and remain until the coming of the Lord, will not precede those who have fallen asleep. For the Lord Himself will descend from heaven with a shout, with the voice of the archangel and with the trumpet of God, and the dead in Christ will rise first. Then we who are alive and remain will be caught up together with then in the clouds to meet the Lord in the air, and so we shall always be with the Lord."

This is a very clear picture of Christ coming back one day to gather up all the dead as well as those who are living. Yes, there will be some who do not die a physical death, but we don't know who because we don't know the time that Christ is coming back.

"But of that day and hour no one knows, not even the angels of heaven, nor the Son, but the Father alone. For the coming of the Son of Man will be just like the days of Noah. For as in those days before the flood they were eating and drinking, marrying and giving in marriage, until the day that Noah entered the ark, and they did not understand until the flood came and took them all away; so will the coming of the Son of Man be" (Matthew 24:36-39).

Have you ever been standing in the check-out line in the grocery store and looked over to see the magazines that have *"The World is Coming to an End"* written on them. We have some in this world who think they can predict when the earth will end. How foolish of them to think they know more than Jesus. We are told that even Jesus doesn't know the hour or the day of the second coming.

In Matthew chapter 25, Jesus tells a parable of 10 virgins who are waiting for the bridegroom. While they are waiting they fall asleep, and then someone yells that the bridegroom is coming. The 10 virgins rise up and get their lamps ready; however, only 5 have oil for their lamps. The other 5 had not gotten ready for the coming of the bridegroom, and they were left out of the wedding feast. This is how the coming of Jesus will be. We will not know when, but we must be ready.

"For we must all appear before the judgment seat of Christ, so that each one may be recompensed for his deeds in the body, according to what he has done, whether good or bad" (2 Corinthians 5:10, 11).

We are all going to have to stand before the judgment seat of Christ. We will not have our mothers or fathers there with us. We won't have friends there with us. It will be just you or just me standing there before the perfect Judge.

We can read the account of the apostle John in the book of Revelation chapter 20 verses 11-15.

As a whole, most Americans don't like to think of the Judgment Day being this way. We like to think most people will be going to heaven because the majority profess to love God; however, just "loving" God, as most define it, is not enough. You must have more. You must have an active love that leads to obedience. Jesus said in John 14:15, *"If you love Me, you will keep My commandments."*

There are basically two meanings to the second coming of Jesus Christ. One is for Christians, those who have been obedient to the Word of God. The other is for non-Christian, those who have not obeyed the Word of God. Let's look at these two separately by looking at the account of the Rich Man and Lazarus in Luke 16:19-31.

1) Non-Christian

There was a rich man who always dressed in nice clothes and lived life in luxury every day. He would pass by the poor and not take care of them, even though he was so richly blessed. One day he died. His destination was Hades. We read in verse 24, *"Father Abraham, have mercy on me, and send Lazarus so that he may dip the tip of his finger in water and cool off my tongue, for I am in agony in this flame."*

2) Christian

The other man in this account is named Lazarus. He was very poor and feeble. We know that he would be placed outside the rich man's gate with hopes he could get just the crumbs from the table. He was so bad off that the dogs licked his sores.

Lazarus died and was carried away by the angels to Abraham's bosom. He was not poor anymore. He was not lying by the gate as a beggar. He didn't have sores to be licked by dogs. He was safe in Abraham's bosom.

lessons learned

1) The Judgment Day is coming.

There are some days in life you just count on. Sunday roles around every 7 days, your birthday happens every year, and the first day of school is going to happen if you're ready or not. Judgment Day is also one of those days you can count on. It's coming.

2) You will be judged.

No matter how fast you are, you can't outrun your own mistakes. At your stage in life, moms, dads, teachers, friends, siblings all seem to find out when you've messed up. If they love you, you're held accountable. Spiritually speaking, when you leave this earth, you will be judged as well. You can't outrun your sins. Your only hope is found in Jesus and the salvation God offers you through Him.

recap

The subject of sin is a serious topic for all those who have reached the age to understand what it means to go against the will of God. The separation that is caused because of our decisions and actions is so wide and serious, God had to send His Son, Jesus, to die on the cross. The bridge was built, allowing us to come back to God. That way is through obedience to Jesus Christ. It involves submission to His will. The Judgment Day is real. You need to make sure you are ready for that last great trial.

questions for thought

1. Does being a "good" person by the world's standards get you to heaven?

2. If the Lord were to come back today, in what category would you be found, saved or lost?

3. If you're in the lost category, would you do anything you could to change that? Why?

4. Do you want to have your sins washed away today? If so, are you willing to talk to your parents, your minister, or Bible class teacher about it?

www.ingramcontent.com/pod-product-compliance
Lightning Source LLC
Chambersburg PA
CBHW050543300426
44113CB00012B/2246